How To Influence People

I0482280

HTeBooks

Copyright © 2016

Copyright © 2016 HTeBooks

All rights reserved. This book or any portion thereof may not be reproduced or used in any manner whatsoever without the express written permission of the publisher except for the use of brief quotations in a book review.

Disclaimer

This book is designed to provide condensed information. It is not intended to reprint all the information that is otherwise available, but instead to complement, amplify and supplement other texts. You are urged to read all the available material, learn as much as possible and tailor the information to your individual needs.

Every effort has been made to make this book as complete and as accurate as possible. However, there may be mistakes, both typographical and in content. Therefore, this text should be used only as a general guide and not as the ultimate source of information. The purpose of this book is to educate.

The author or the publisher shall have neither liability nor responsibility to any person or entity with respect to any loss or damage caused, or alleged to have been caused, directly or indirectly, by the information contained in this book.

Table of Contents

Introduction

We are all in need of effective communication and persuasion skills.

Communication and persuasion skills are essential whether you are in business, sales and marketing or politics. You need them for your professional, social and personal life. Strong bonds and sturdy relationships are built on communication. And your ability to negotiate is constantly tested in everyday life.

People influence each other every single day. We are filled with emotions, opinions and ideas and it is in our nature to feel compelled to share them. But it is not just about expressing such thoughts and emotions. We also have to think about the best way to approach other people.

Each of us is unique in our own ways. We have many differences. And if we focus on those differences, we will never be able to move forward or even live together in harmony. Although we may have a few similarities, we have to bank on those because those are essential in building a harmonious life together.

But why do some people seem to be more effective than others? Do you ever wonder why some people seem to always get what they want? What makes them different?

Skills are not things you are born with. These are things we can all learn. So, if you feel like you are not a great communicator or think that you have zero persuasion skills, you have to stop fretting. You can harness these skills.

The good news is you have picked out the right book.

Do you want to find out the secrets of the best communicators and persuaders of our time? Are you aiming for improvement? Do you want to succeed? If you do, read on.

1. Leave Your Worries and Fears at the Door

You cannot enter the room carrying the weight of your fears and worries. The slightest hint of hesitation will give you away. If you are unsure about yourself and what you are trying to propose then the people listening to you will feel the same way. Unless you are 100% confident and certain about your offer, you cannot give them the same assurance.

So, shake off all worries and fears that your attempt at persuading your audience may not go as you hope it to be. When you worry about failing, it has a negative impact on your attempt. Moreover, such feelings of fear and worry only act as obstacles for your improvement.

Do not think about making mistakes or being unsuccessful. It may be easier said than done. But if you practice enough, you will gain self-confidence. This is why you have to work at convincing yourself first that success is possible. The more you believe it then you will come across as more convincing.

Avoid entertaining negative thoughts. Make no room for such negative feelings. They will only affect your mood. They may only take your hopes down. Worry and fear will only make you more nervous than you already are. These emotions will make you appear stiff. And ultimately, it will have a negative impact on how people perceive you, the same people you are trying to persuade in joining your cause.

Of course, no one is immune to making mistakes. Everybody makes them at one point or another. After all, nobody is perfect. While you may not be able to avoid mistakes or any mishaps during your presentation and the discussion after, one thing is for sure. You can make the most out of that experience by learning from it. This is the best way to improve your persuasion and communication skills.

Mistakes, as long as you learn from them, can make you better and better. So in the future, you come out stronger and better skilled at communicating and persuading your audience. So, mistakes may seem like a disaster today. But it prepares you for the future. Do not be afraid to make them.

Believe that you can do it!

2. Learn to Listen

Communication and persuasion are not just about talking or listening to your own voice. Although the manner of speaking, the choice of words, your tone and voice projection are all important elements, listening is also a quality you need to develop. You can make people listen when you also show that you are listening to them. Pay attention to their concerns and do not just be engrossed with your own. When you pay attention to what they have to say, you give yourself better chances of getting them on your side.

You may be surprised at how much people are willing to give away. If only you take the time to listen. So if you want to improve your persuasion and communication skills, you have to learn to listen carefully first. Communication after all is a two way street. To be heard, you have to listen too. That makes communication fruitful.

Give the other person a chance to tell you and express all that he needs and wants. Listen intently to what he has to say. Take note of the hints he is dropping. When you have a better idea of his needs and wants, you can better tailor your argument to fit into his circumstances. It gives you a better chance to help this person. That is what persuasion is all about. This is what makes it so different from manipulation.

On one hand, manipulation is about using the knowledge you have picked up or the people you encounter only as means to realize your own goals and pursue your own interests. Persuasion on the other hand, is about not only being concerned about your own interests. It is about creating a win-win situation where both parties benefit.

This is why it is so important to listen as it is the only way for you to learn the other person's interest. Otherwise you will sound and appear self-centered. And the last thing you want is to make the other person feel used and manipulated.

You already know what you want and need. So, take the time to find out what the other party wants and needs as well. Keep in mind that everybody strives for benefits. Make it your goal to achieve benefits for both sides. The only way to do that is to listen intently and carefully.

3. Persuade Only the Persuadable

The best persuaders and communicators in the world make it seem like it is quite easy to get people on their sides. They have this fascinating charisma that make people want to listen and follow them. But even these individuals recognize the fact that only the persuadable can truly be persuaded.

Do not get it wrong; everybody can be persuaded but only if you find the right timing and the proper context. Even the hardest shell can be cracked given time. If you have all the time in the world then by all means go ahead and target everyone. However, for the short term, it is not wise to randomly choose your audience.

Define your target market. Get to know them, their motivations and what influences them. Dig deeper into their psyche. More importantly, find out if these people can be swayed. Otherwise, you may only end up wasting your time and effort.

This is the first step at persuasion. That is to find the people you can be persuaded to adopt your own point of view. Once you find them, make you're your primary target. Focus your effort and attention to them.

Remember that you may only fail at getting through to someone who is not even interested in what you have to say. The truth is people are most interested in themselves. Most people spend a lot of time pondering upon matters of love, money and health. But if you figure out the right approach and become consistent at your method focusing on their areas of concern, you may be able to get their attention.

Persuading them however, is a different matter. It may take longer than you expect. So the best way to do this is to craft a different approach for these people. And set proper expectations. They require a different timeline, one that may be longer. And for that, you need to be very patient.

4. Be a Storyteller

The most skilled communicators and persuaders are also great storytellers. That is because great stories have the power to get the listeners involved as if they are a part of the story. Stories create an experience not only for the characters but also for the people you share it with. They create an emotional connection with the audience. And appealing to the emotions is one of the most effective methods of persuasion and communication.

This is why you have to learn the art of storytelling. More importantly, you have to learn how to tell remarkable stories. You can use stories to send the message across. It is a subtle way of selling and convincing the audience. People have the tendency to turn their backs the minute they figure out what you are trying to do, selling that is. But by making a connection first through stories, they become more open to the idea or to what you have to offer.

The human brain becomes more concerned with taking pleasure in the story and at the same time pondering upon the message. This means the persuasion attempt gets under the radar.

Keep in mind that the manner by which you say something is equally important as the message itself. Stories make a great method at communication and persuasion as they are much easier to understand. They are also easier to relate to. Through stories, people share and interpret experiences. And it is remarkable experiences that can sway people's beliefs. Great stories have the power to change the way people view the world.

Stories also encourage dialogue. And when you are trying to communicate or persuade someone, you want to engage them. You want them to interact with you. Many high budgeted marketing campaigns fail because they disregard one of the most important elements. That is meaningful context. When you relentlessly push your message without considering relevancy to the market, you will likely face a loss. But if you build the context first and make it meaningful to your audience, you have a better chance at convincing people.

You can absolutely use stories as a way of presenting your message. And as experience proves, it is an effective method of persuasion and communication. Remember that people act with resistance when they get the impression of being pushed to do something. They do not like other people telling them what they need or want. However, they will find it irresistible to agree with a message when it is presented through a great story. They find it easier to agree with the moral of the story. And the agreement does not hurt their pride.

5. Be the First to Give

When people do something for another, they always think of what they can get in return. The ideal human relationship if based on giving and taking. But more often than not, people like the assurance of being able to receive something in return before they even give something. That is the human nature.

But studies also show that people are more likely to succumb at a persuasion attempt when the persuader has done something for them first. Think about it. When another person did you a favour in the past and when he comes back running to you for help years later, you are likely to remember the help this person has extended to you before. And because of that favour, you will feel compelled to do something for this person in return.

It does not even matter whether it is a small act of kindness or a life changing gesture. It has the same effect. It triggers a response. Again, that is because of the give and take relationship that people adhere to.

People are not responsive to telemarketers because they know this caller wants to take something from them. The telemarketer wants them to say yes to the offer. This makes people more hesitant to agree. And even if the offer is good enough, they will still act with resistance.

So, the next time you make an attempt to persuade someone, try to do something for this person first. Instead of taking away from them, be the first to give. It does not necessarily have to be a huge act. A favour can come in small acts too. And it can invoke the same kind of response.

Moreover, make your request personal. According to studies, personalized requests are more effective in invoking a positive response. They are more persuasive. So, customize your approach. Be personable. Make your interactions and messages more personal. It further establishes the connection. And you will find that people respond to such an approach in a more positive way.

6. Limit the Choices

As humans, we all have pride. We are proud that we make our own decisions and that we act independently. The truth is we are influenced by a lot of factors all the time. These influencers have a huge impact on our decision making process. And it is true whether we care to admit it or not.

And so we do not like the idea of being bossed around. We do not like other people deciding for us. We do not like them telling us what to do or what we should do. The minute we get such an impression, we are most likely to turn our backs. You have to keep this in mind when you are working to improve your communication and persuasion skills.

With that said, you have to give your audience the power of choice. Be careful not to rob them off that power. Avoid telling them what they should do. In the end, you have to emphasize it is they who will decide. You can offer suggestions without pushing too hard because that will only make them more resistant. Make sure to offer them choices.

While choices are important, you should also avoid giving them too many. People do like to have options. But that does not mean you have to offer them so many. This will only make it much more difficult for them to make a decision. It will cause information overload and that will only lead to confusion. Your audience will only get frustrated. You certainly would not want that to happen.

Give them enough options but never too much. People do better with only a few options available. Consider the case of companies that only offer a few retirement plans versus those that offer such a large number of retirement plan options. The companies that only have a few tend to have higher number of enrollment.

Simplicity is the key. Give your audience the power of choice but make it simple enough. This will prompt them to make choices. Otherwise, they get confused, frustrated and eventually give up. Faced with too many options, too much to think about, people are likely to not make any choices at all.

7. Go against Self-Interest

Trust is a critical factor in building a relationship. In dealing with others, establishing trust is crucial. And it also makes an essential element of persuasion. And so if you want to become more persuasive, you have to work at establishing trust first. You have to learn how to gain people's trust. Otherwise, you are in trouble.

The thing is it is not easy to earn trust. People do not exactly give it away. They cling onto it tighter than anything they own. And their grip even gets tauter when they are faced with someone who is trying to get on their good side. This makes it much more difficult to sway people. But it does not make it such an impossible feat.

So, how do you exactly earn people's trust?

When you are trying to persuade people, always keep this in mind. Nothing and no one is perfect. People know this fact as well. Even the best offers in the world have a catch. And it is likely that yours has some too.

People have now become smarter. They have become immune to marketing ploys. They have learned to read between the lines, to expect a flaw from a seemingly perfect deal. Your job is not to make the offer flawless. It is not your job to present it in such a perfect way or make it sound like it is too good to be true. Rather, your job is to make the offer real. And it is real when it is flawed.

Just because something has a negative side does not make it all bad. This means you have to point out the offer's weaknesses before your audience figure it out themselves. You have to lay it on the table. This will be perceived as honesty. You do not have to bash your own product or whatever it is you are trying to offer, you just have to be truthful about it.

More often than not, pointing out the weakness in your offer, product or argument immediately before presenting the strengths make people more receptive. Because of this, you give them the impression that you have their best interest in mind. By not sugarcoating the truth about your offer, you have better chances of earning their trust. And when you have their trust, you have better chances of persuading them.

8. Establish Your Credibility

Exactly how crucial is credibility? Think about this for a second. Would you go to a convention about profitable investment advice when Bernie Madoff was the speaker? Would you listen to tips for dressing professionally or appropriately when Lady Gaga was the one who offers it? Would you attend a convention about maintaining marriage fidelity when John Edwards was the speaker?

You probably would not. And that is simply because these individuals are the opposite of what they offer to advise you in. If you are to listen to some advice, the first thing you consider is the reliability or the credibility of the source. Does this person know what he or she is talking about? Would you trust his or her words about the matter?

Aristotle cited three crucial elements of persuasion. These are logic, emotions and credibility. According to him, credibility is the most important. He said the speaker's credibility may almost be called the most effective means of persuasion he possesses." In which case, you have to work in building and maintaining your credibility first.

How do you do this exactly? Here are some suggestions.

Establish expertise on the topic.

Before even speak to the audience, it is important that you demonstrate how or why they should listen to what you have to say about a topic. For instance, if you are speaking about entrepreneurial opportunity, your audience has to be informed about your educational background or your entrepreneurial experience. They have to be told about other credentials under your name or just about anything that helps build your credibility as a speaker, your reliability to speak about the topic or simply why these people have to trust your words about the matter.

If you are being introduced before the audience, make sure the person making the introduction mentions these things. It is better it comes from another person's mouth rather than yours so it sounds more trustworthy.

Do a Meet and Greet

Apply a personal approach. Not only will your audience get to know you and possibly form a positive impression of you. This way, you also get the opportunity to get to know some of them. This will give you more ideas on how to sway them on your side or simply to capture their interests.

Build Credibility by Association

Another effective way of building credibility is through association. Remember what they say about birds of the same feather flocking together. This does not necessarily mean you must only hangout with people who share the same expertise. Rather, this is especially applicable to the way you quote authorities in the subject matter specifically those who are widely recognized on the subject matter.

This shall demonstrate your familiarity with the best practices of such experts. This is a way of associating yourself with these so called experts. And in a way, it also enhances your authority in the topic.

Always demonstrate good taste.

Respect is earned. And if you want respect from your audience, you have to be willing to work hard to earn it. Jokes can be used to build rapport. But again, do not overstep your boundaries. Avoid racy remarks or distasteful comments about sensitive topics. Show respect.

9. Establish Common Ground

In addition to credibility, there are plenty of other crucial variables that play a role in the success or failure of your attempts at getting through to people. It takes more than first impressions to convince people to take a new position or a contrary one. And one of the essential things you have to do is to establish common ground.

You have to present your idea, product or service in a way that emphasizes the shared benefits. Do you think you can convince a man on the street when all you talk about is how this idea can benefit you? It is doubtful this person will even give you the time.

To persuade people and to communicate with them effectively, you have to speak their language to. Talk in terms of how the idea can be advantageous to them too. Get your audience involved. You can secure their commitment to what you have to offer as long as you work in helping them understand the potential benefits they can acquire from pushing the same idea or accepting it in the same way that you do.

All it takes is proper framing of your statements and arguments. It is about focusing on facts that further support your claims. And to determine the right framing strategy, you need an in-depth understanding of your target. This means you have to spend time and effort in preparation. That includes collecting information. You can acquire information by developing excellent listening skills. People will drop hints about the important things to them. And you can design your approach by working around their interests and goals.

Another way of figuring out what works is through testing. You have to know how people would react to your presentation or proposal. You can do this by making the presentation to your trusted coworkers.

Do not just make statements. Statements can be powerful but asking questions is quite effective as well in getting your audience involved. Consider the perceptions of your audience. Take the time to assess your arguments and your corresponding evidences.

Come up with a compromise. Make sure you find that common ground that links you to your audience. Make an effort for them to recognize that it is in their best interest to accept this new or contrary idea. Let them know and feel you are not only working for your own selfish interests. Rather, you also have their best interest in mind.

10. Pay Attention to the Accuracy of Facts

After establishing credibility and common ground, it is equally crucial to straighten out the argument with the straight facts.

People will not just trust you for your words. You need to prove that what you are offering is beneficial to their cause. To do that, you must present them with sufficient and strong evidence. This shall support your statements.

Pieces of evidence can help explain why what you are offering is important or how it will affect your audience. You need to give them a good reason to follow your advice, to take your side or take the direction you are trying to steer them into. It is your responsibility to build the case. That is how you can persuade people.

We have mentioned previously about the importance of using emotions. Aristotle recognizes it as one of the three elements of persuasion. However, you should not just rely on emotional appeal alone. People always look for a logical reason.

Make sure that your argument is logical. Provide the reasons supporting your position or your argument. Without logical reasoning, your claims are deemed baseless and undermined.

When you do present them with vivid evidence, make sure that it is filled with facts and not just any facts. They must be first and foremost, accurate.

Accuracy is another crucial element that is crucial in establishing your credibility and therefore essential in persuasion. When you lay down facts, be sure to check on them first. Make sure they are true and accurate

Double-check on the facts you present. Make sure your statements are accurate. Remember than a single incorrect or inaccurate statement can make people question your credibility. So go the extra to ensure it does not happen.

When we talk about evidence, we are not just referring to numeric data although these are important too. Take note from the techniques of the most excellent persuaders.

Learn the ability to connect numbers with stories. Provide examples. Use metaphors and analogies. These things can make your presentation much more engaging. And that can help with regard to capturing and sustaining the interest of your audience in the subject matter.

The bottom line is people notice everything. They build impressions about you from the way you speak to how you interact, from the way you move to how you make eye contact. Whatever they think about you has a huge impact on what they think about whatever it is you are presenting. This is why you have to make it one of your priorities to build and maintain high credibility and strengthen that further with accuracy.

11. Avoid Bridging

Persuading is not just about presenting your position and the corresponding arguments and facts to support it. Effective communication is always a two-way street. That said you must also take the time to hear out comments and questions. And your chances of getting through to your audience depend a lot on the way you answer their questions. And whatever you do, you must make it a point to resist the temptation of resorting to bridging.

Bridging is a technique used by individuals who either does not know how to answer a question or simply clueless about the right answer. When someone asks you a question, do not resort to bridging or dodging the question and making an attempt to switch the focus on a topic that is safer to discuss.

While it is important that your audience get the impression that you know what you are talking about, that you are an expert, there is no shame in admitting that you are not all knowing. Some people can use this technique incredibly so much so that it becomes almost undetected. However, it is a risky move. And it can hurt more than help your cause.

When you are not sure about the answer or you are completely clueless about it, do not be afraid to admit it. But then, tell your audience that you will look it up. Take that promise seriously. Make sure you do look it up and provide a satisfactory answer. This is another way of showing just how you take the matter seriously. It is also a way of conveying your commitment and sincerity.

Never underestimate the ability of the audience to spot a diversion. They can sense one. And when they sense that you are making one, they will certainly lose interest. What's worse is that this can make them retaliate. And once they turn their back on you, it will prove much more difficult and almost impossible to get them to listen again.

12. Use Emotional Appeal but Maintain Emotional Stability

Aristotle cited emotions as one of the key elements of persuasion in addition to credibility. And expressing emotions can be helpful in boosting your credibility as well. However, the matter is quite tricky.

Leaning to an emotional appeal can be quite powerful. Rational and objective approach to the matter is essential. But more often than not, logic is not enough to win a case. This is not to say that emotions are more important than presenting a set of clear and logical evidence. But combining both logic and emotions can do the job.

Reach out to your audience. Dig deep into their emotions and psyches. Get to know their fears, their hopes and frustrations. Understand their hates and loves. Find out what their emotional button is. You can use such information in figuring out the best way to say what you want to say in a way that they will agree with you.

Emotions can be very helpful to your cause. However, it has to be done properly and appropriately. Be aware of your boundaries. Do not make the mistake of going beyond it. Otherwise, it is difficult to go back.

Some effective persuaders are quite capable of using their emotions in such an effective manner. In some cases, persuaders use the emotion of anger purposefully and it works to their advantage. You can do it too. However, you should never lose self-control. And do not overdo it. If you are to use anger, use it sparingly.

Remember the quality of the most recognized leaders. In the face of conflict, they are the ones who remain calm and emotionally detached. And people are more likely to listen to someone who is thinking clearly, who is not clouded by emotions.

13. Emphasize on Possible Losses More Than Potential Gains

The value of things is relative. It means people want things because other people have it except of course for the necessities. And such want for such things increase when only a few people can have it. In other words, scarcity can make people go at great lengths to avail of something.

It is all about the idea of exclusivity. In which case, creating scarcity can contribute to your persuasion success. If you want people to want what you have, you need to make it scarce. And that also applies even to your own self.

Moreover, several studies show that people respond more on possible losses than potential gains. In fact, there is a formulated theory with regard to this phenomenon and it is referred to as loss aversion. Loss aversion refers to the tendency in individuals to prefer the avoidance of losses and focus less on the acquisition of gains.

Do not get it wrong; presenting potential gains can be effective to. However, as some studies show, losses prove to be twice as powerful. The idea of losing something, which is deemed valuable, has a stronger psychological effect on people. In which case, they become more responsive. They are more ready to take action in order to prevent or at least lessen the possibility of such a loss twice as much as they would than acquiring a potential gain.

Based on the loss aversion theory, avoiding a $5 surcharge is more urgent than getting a $5 discount. It is all about framing your statement so that the possible loss is more emphasized. You can tell people what they stand to gain from buying a product, following your advice or sharing your position. But according to various research, individuals are more persuaded when they are told what they stand to lose out on when they do not buy a product, follow a piece of advice or disregard an opinion.

Take the case of the Oldsmobile brand. In 2003, the brand earned far more than the sales projections considering there was an extremely slow sales prior to the increase. And General Motors even implemented budget cut backs on advertising and product development.

So how did they manage to do it? The company had decided to discontinue the car due to slow sales. This made the car face potential scarcity. It turned the car into something that people will possibly lose out on. And when people learned about the news, they acted on preventing the loss. It was a sweet gain for the company.

It is something worth thinking about. And it is absolutely worth applying for the sake of improving your results.

14. Appeal to the Subject's Self-Interest

For people the most interest thing in the world is their own stories. When you are trying to persuade someone you have to keep this in mind.

One of the biggest questions people have in their minds is "What's in it for me?" Your chances of success depend on how well you answer this question, on how satisfying that answer will be.

People are not always ready to be selfless. More often than not, they are not willing to grant your request unless you have done something important for them too or if there is something they stand to gain from granting such a request. Human behavior is focused on satisfying self-interest. And this is something you have to understand even before you lay your cards and demands on the table.

Before you put yourself out there, you have to learn and understand what is it that makes people tick. You have to figure out their sweet spots. And you have to hit the bull's eye when you are making the offer. Do not make any demands yet unless you have already anticipated and have a ready satisfying answer to the big question.

You already know what you stand to gain. But it is equally important to satisfy the interest of the other person. When you appeal to your subject's self interest in an effective manner, you have better chances of persuading them.

15. Tailor Your Argument to the Listener

You also have to understand that not everyone is the same. Every individual is unique. And this means people have unique and different needs, goals, fears, aspirations and interests. In other words, what may have worked for one does not necessarily work for everyone else. What may have persuaded person A may not be necessarily good enough for person B.

Before you make your presentation, you have to know who you are talking to. Get to know the person's or this group's needs, goals, interests, aspirations and fears. Are they all the same? Probably not. In which case, you have to tailor your argument and frame your statements in a way that corresponds to this subject's uniqueness.

You have to go beyond the obvious. Demographic facts do not define the individuality of a person. Understand what motivates your audience. Read into their behavior and psyche.

Other matters such as the level of the individual's knowledge about the subject matter and their preconceived views are also worth knowing. You have to determine whether or not such preconceived views aligned with yours. Find out how this particular individual wants to be treated or addressed. Determine this person's behavioral style. Knowing these things is the key to identifying the best persuasion strategy that can draw out a favorable response.

16. Build an Organized Pattern

The idea is clear to you. Now, you have to find a way to present it to your audience well so it becomes clear to them as well.

It does not matter how huge the idea is or how beneficial it is for your audience. Unless you present it clearly, it is a waste. Your main objective should be to make them understand and to avoid confusing them because confusion often leads to frustration. And it does not just apply to you, but more importantly, it applies to them too.

To achieve success, you have to make your presentation clear. And in order to do that, you have to know exactly what it is that you want to accomplish provided that your attempt to persuade is a success. Define your goals. And this should serve as your guide in crafting your presentation. Use this as reference when you outline your arguments. Use this as basis for framing your statements.

When you present your points, do so one at a time. Avoid bombarding the audience with ideas that do not necessarily go together. It may make sense to you but for an audience that is clueless, it would all sound gibberish.

Write a draft. Edit out unnecessary points. Group together the ideas that support each other. Be clear and precise in your statements. Proofread. Make it perfect.

Build your arguments. Provide support. Ensure the accuracy of your facts.

Do not jump immediately from one point to another. Always make sure your audience is on the same page. How do you go about it? It is quite simple. That is with the use of transitions.

Transitions are crucial. And you have to make yours flawless. For instance, periodic summaries can help keep your audience engaged. State your points in an organized manner. Repeat points that you want to reiterate. Summarize and make smooth transitions. This will help your audience follow your thoughts. And that takes you a step closer to getting through to them.

17. Be Persistent

The chances of succeeding at the first attempt are slim to none. There are only a very few people who can claim to have succeeded at first try. And mind you, even the most successful people in history have faced seemingly insurmountable obstacles before they had their first taste of success.

What does this mean for you? Just because you have not succeeded in your first try at persuading some people does not necessarily mean you are doomed. You are not a hopeless case. Rather than dwelling in misery, treat the experience only as a setback.

Learn what you can from it. Use it to improve your communication and persuasion skills. Determine your weak points. Work at improving them. Sustain your strengths.

Keep this in mind. The person who keeps asking for what they want and does not stop demonstrating the value of what it is they are offering is likely to persuade people. Be persistent and it will happen eventually.

Take the case of Abraham Lincoln. Before he became a historical figure and touched the lives of the masses, he went through many losses starting with the loss of his mother then his three sons then eight elections and more. He failed in his business. He had his share of personal failures. He faced defeat before he was elected as the United States president. But in the face of his losses and failures, he remained true to his message. He persisted in his endeavors. He did not give up easily.

You may face countless "NO's" before you hear a "YES." Doors may close in your face. People may ignore you. But when you meet that first person who lends an ear, who cares to sit and hear you out, that person who gives you a chance and lets you hear the sweetest "YES," you know your efforts, the amount of time and energy you put into your work are all worth it.

So, do not give up just yet. Keep on improving your skills. Work harder. Try and try again. Soon enough, you will have your reward.

And all the hardships and challenges that were thrown your way make the reward so much sweeter. You will triumph but you have to be patient and persistent.

18. Ask and Keep Asking, Never Assume

Assumptions are detrimental to your attempt at persuasion. Whatever you do, you must resist the temptation to assume matters about your audience.

For instance, how many sales personnel pass up the opportunity to land a successful sale simply because they have made the assumption that their target market lacks the money, resources or interest about their product or service? How many marketing campaigns have become wastes of money because marketers have assumed their target cares about certain things which they in truth, never cross their target's minds?

This is one of the biggest reasons why you must work at preparation and planning. Prepare by collecting as much valuable information as you can about your target audience. This shall determine the success or failure of your communication and persuasion efforts.

Know more about these people. Familiarize yourself with situations that happen around you. You must be willing to get out of your comfort zone and think outside the box if you want to succeed at communicating effectively and persuading your target audience.

Targeting everyone is not wise. But it is not smart either to jump into conclusions that certain people do not have a care about your offer. This is why you need to do research to find out for sure. Do not hold back from making an offer because of your baseless assumptions. These are not good enough reason to avoid making the effort.

If you want to be certain, all you have to do is to simply ask. Make the offer. Present the idea anyway. Give it your best shot. You must let the decision come from your subject. Leave the choice to them at least you have tried than not make an attempt at all and run the risk of losing on an opportunity.

The most effective persuasion strategies are a product of months and even years of meticulous preparation. Think about it. Do you think you have equal chances of acing a job interview if you know nothing about the company or position you are applying for or if you are well versed in the company's background and the position's demands? Undoubtedly, preparation gives you due advantage.

19. Create Urgency

We have talked previously about the advantages of creating scarcity. We have emphasized on the powerful effect of focusing on what people stand to lose rather than on what they stand to gain. And in addition to scarcity, you also need to stir a sense of urgency.

Some people need more push than others. While some people can be persuaded in a short period of time, it may take more for others. You have to wait for that right moment to get them to act and grant your request or give you idea, product or service a chance. But if you are working on a tight schedule, you may need to do some magic. And such magic does not involve waving a wand or chanting spells. It involves creating the right motivation.

If you want your target audience to act right away, you must determine their motivations. You also need to understand their decision making process. It is important that you identify which step they are actually in so you can direct your actions, your presentation and arguments in a way that takes them a step closer to saying "YES."

Remember the Oldsmobile brand and how they picked up sales because of the news the company released on pulling out the car? The company probably set a deadline. And people have become aware of that. When people got hold of the news, they were compelled not only of the idea of the car being scarce. They were also quite aware that soon they would not have the chance to get it. This was enough to motivate them to act immediately and so they did.

If you want to instill a sense of urgency, if you want your subjects to act and decide right away, you have to motivate them to.

20. Paint a Picture

Images do matter. The most effective communicators and persuaders have the ability to pain the picture to their audience. They do not just speak sweet words. Their presentations are more compelling because they use images as well.

We are not referring to literal images in the presentation. Rather, what we are referring to is the ability to make the offer more real by letting your target audience see the picture and experience the scenario in their minds. And visualizations can be more powerful than pictures visible to the eyes only.

When you build your presentation and present your arguments, do not just settle for bullet lists. Rather, make it more interesting by using a combination of presentation techniques. Avoid boring your audience with a monotonous presentation. What you need to do is spark up their presentation. And you do well know bullet points are not enough to do the job.

When you speak about benefits and advantages, do not just present it in a list. Talk from their perspective. For instance, do not talk about how a cleaning product has certain ingredients that make it a more effective cleaning tool. If you want your audience to relate, you need a more personal approach than that. So, talk about how the homemaker has extra time to play with her kids when she uses the cleaning product.

It is much simpler to say the cleaning product can save your target time or that the product is twice as effective as other brands, which make cleaning fast. But it has lesser ring to it. It is more effective to let the target imagine what his or her life will be like if he or she decides to use your product. What can your subject do with that extra time? Based on your target's motivation, paint the scenario so that they can see with their minds' eyes. Provide them the experience.

Paint it so that it becomes more vivid. Emphasize on that future beneficial experience that you can give them through your offer. Describe it to them so the picture becomes clearer. Once they are able to visualize, they become more open to considering what you have to offer and finally making the jump you are asking them to make.

21. Just Tell the Truth

People lie all the time. They sue lies as means to getting what they want. It is fascinating how people think of marketers and advertisers as liars. And being bombarded with exaggerated claims all the time makes it understandable how they have come up with such conclusions.

When you are being offered something, whether it is a new idea, product, service or position, your thoughts jump to thinking about the catch behind the offer. Your mind begins to wonder almost immediately which statements are lies. And you probably are doubtful about the truthfulness of the sales personnel's statements. You laugh at the thought that this sales person thinks you are close to being convinced. You find it amusing how this person who is making the offer think you are that foolish to fall for his or her trap of lies.

Think about this scenario. Now, think about how your audience thinks the same thoughts when you are blabbering endlessly about your idea. It definitely sucks but it is true. If it happens to you, it certainly happens to someone else. The worst part is what if that someone else is the person you are working hard to persuade.

The point is people have become so used to hearing lies. They expect it every time someone approaches them with an offer or a request. They have become so immune to lies that they have developed a shield. They are unaffected. They may seem listening but their minds are wandering off somewhere. And so it becomes a delightful surprise when they hear the truth for a change.

You do not have to lie to persuade someone. In fact, telling a lie will only make you lose your chance. People will flatter another to get what they want. And the receiver can tell whether the remark is genuine or if it is just a ploy to get them to listen.

If you want people to hear you out, simply tell them the truth. This does not mean you have to be nasty. But dare tell them something other people do not have the guts to tell them about themselves. It can be a tricky and risky situation because the truth is often unpleasant. But when you tell the truth without a grace of judgment, without an agenda, you may become surprised at how people will respond to your honesty.

After all, you need to earn their trust before you can get through to them. And you can certainly earn their trust by being true and real.

22. Build Rapport

We respond to people whom we think we share common interests and goals with. We relate better with people that we like. It is not a conscious decision but it definitely affects our unconscious behaviors. So, if you want to amp your chances of getting through to your audience, you must work at learning how to build rapport with them.

Rapport is defined as a state of harmonious understanding between people. This understanding paves the way to better and easier communication. It happens with people who seem to hit it off instantly.

So, how do you exactly get on well with your audience?

If you find such commonality, your communication becomes much more effective. Rapport can be built in several ways including the following.

Mirror the other person's body language.

You do not have to be a wizard to figure out a person's body language. You just have to be observant. Take note of the other person's posture and body movements. Avoid copying it in the moment as such may make you appear annoyingly strange. Rather, wait for a few seconds before you shift your movement or posture in the same way.

You also need to note the subject's gestures. When it is your turn to talk, apply the same hand gestures as the other person did. And when it comes to facial expressions, make sure that you match those instantly. For instance, if the other person raises his or her eyebrows, you have to raise yours too. It is a way of acknowledging the other person's emotion. When the other person uses head nods, make sure to nod your head as well to show your agreement.

Copy the other person's tonality.

You have to be more observant when it comes to accents, volume and depth of voice. But you have to be extra careful when you mimic accents. The last thing you want is to give the impression that you are mocking the other person's accent. Instead of literally copying it, you may want to take note of specific words and how the other person pronounces it.

Also, you must match the volume level of your subject. Do not be louder or softer. Finally, match the other person's voice depth. Figure out where the voice is coming from whether from the throat, chest or nose.

Match the other person's breathing pattern.

Another important element you have to pay attention to is the way the other person breathes. While talking to this person, breathe in the same way they breathe. When your breathing pattern matches, it results to a hypnotic synchronization.

Match the other person's rate of speech.

Does the other person talk fast or slow? Remember that a fast rate of speech is usually associated with a salesman or woman and this raises a red flag in some people. So, you have to be extra conscious.

On the other hand, a person who talks very slowly is often thought off as unintelligent. And you would not want to make that impression. Unless the other person talks that way, avoid doing so. Instead, make sure you speak in a steady rate.

It is also quite important to be sensitive about your subject's rhythm of speech. Take note if they have bursts. If they speak in a steady rhythm, make sure you do too.

Acknowledge by repetition

It is one of the simplest ways of building rapport. But it is surprising how so many people tend to forget it. Take note of the important things the other person pointed out. You have to make sure this person knows you were listening intently. When it is your turn to talk, provide a brief synopsis of what he or she has just said.

Finally, to build rapport you must assume that you already have built one with the other person. Talk to your audience as you would talk to your trusted friends. This way, you send subconscious signals. And it can be very encouraging in a way that will make the other person view you in the same way.

23. Practice Behavioral Flexibility

Behavioral flexibility is defined as the ability to change one's actions when the current actions seem insufficient at achieving the results one is aiming for. It is the ability to do things differently. And it requires that you step out of your comfort zone.

Behavioral flexibility is not just important for communicators and persuaders. It is crucial to overall success in whatever you choose to do. In fact, what makes people in control is not power. It is their versatility or flexibility. Behavioral flexibility is about adaptability and responding to the change that happens around you.

We can all take lessons from children when it comes to behavioral flexibility. Notice how a child who wants to be bought a toy would go through a series of different behaviors to get what he or she wants. A parent is more likely to stick to saying "No." But a child will not only pout. When pouting does not get the results he or she is aiming for, this child will resort to crying. If that still does not work, he or she would try to bargain. A child will also go at great lengths to plead and beg. He or she would even turn his or her charms on in the hope of convincing the adult to give in.

A child does not give up easily. And children have more than one weapon to get what they want. They have an entire repertoire of behaviors. They know the more they have in the bag is the more chances they have of persuading their moms and dads.

If you want to improve your persuasion and communication skills, you have to think like a child. That is you must not only try and try again. At each try, you must adapt. Do not try the same techniques all the time. Make sure you have a series of tactics.

For instance, if you have framed your statement in a certain way and the other person does not get it, you must try another way of stating your point. Reword it. Make it simpler. Frame it in such a way that the other person will find it relatable. If it does not work still, try using images. Tell a story. Provide examples.

Do not be afraid to try out new things. Try different things. Eliminate self-doubt. Learn from other people, from experts and mentors. Understand their strategies and try them out yourself. Behavioral flexibility encourages you to spread your wings and broaden your horizon. And that is essential in being successful not only with communicating and persuading people but in being successful generally in life.

24. Learn to Transfer Energy

It is fascinating how some people can infuse us with positive energy. And it is amazing how others can drain us of our positive energy by simply being around us. We get energy from other people. In the same way, we influence other people's energies. Most of the time, this transfer of energy occurs unconsciously or subconsciously.

If you want to be successful at persuading and motivating others, you have to learn how to transfer energy. You have to understand how it happens. The most persuasive people have mastered this ability. They have a deep understanding of other people's motivations. They know exactly how to invigorate others. But how do you do this?

You have to start with yourself. You cannot transfer positive energy when you are filled with negativity. Eliminate negative thoughts and emotions. That is easier said than done but it is crucial.

Surround yourself with positive people. Avoid those that drain you out as they will only drag you down. Read inspirational books. Learn from the experts. Meditate. Learn to cope and manage stress. Take care of your health. Eat right and exercise properly.

Do not succumb to doubts, fears and worries. We all have them but it is important that you do not let yourself be defeated by these negative thoughts and emotions. Fill yourself up with positive energy so that you have a lot to give.

So when you have an overflowing positivity, it will show. Other people will feel it from you. There are different ways to transfer energy. It can be as simple as saying encouraging words. It can be done through eye contact. It can travel through laughter and physical touch. The transfer of energy can come in the form of listening. Energy can also be sent through expression of excitement in verbal responses.

Why is it important to pay attention to this? Think about it, would you rather associate yourself with people who are filled with negativity than one who has positive energy? Will you be persuaded by someone who drains you off of your stored energy or one who infuses you with more energy?

25. Be Confident and Certain

Confidence can give you certainty. And both are compelling. Confidence and certain can be both intoxicating. And these are attractive qualities you must adopt if you want to be an effective communicator and a successful persuader.

No one else will believe you unless you come across as confident. If you are doubtful and uncertain, people will read into that. And what chances do you have of getting through to people when you lack confidence and certainty? You probably do not stand a chance. People themselves are doubtful. And you cannot pull them to the other side when you are quite negative as well.

You must have an unbridled sense of certainty if you want to attract several "YES's." You must be confident in what you have to say. You have to be a hundred percent sure what you are offering can be beneficial to your subject's life. You have to believe in your own offer. Otherwise, you cannot expect to lure others into it.

You have to be oozing with confidence but at the same time be careful about coming across as cocky. There is a huge difference. What you want to send out to your audience is positive confidence.

It takes practice to have that kind of confidence. Expose yourself to various situations. Experience can teach you that you have absolutely nothing to be afraid of. And you have to convince other people of the same with your words, with your example. The best way to do that is to work hard at becoming a role model, an image of your message and a positive representation of your cause.

Final Thoughts

At first, it can prove quite difficult to get others on your side. It may even seem impossible to make some people change their minds. They can be resistant. They can resort to retaliation. You may be ignored or shut off.

While it is possible to face rejection, it is also possible to earn acceptance. In which case, you must not give up even before you try. Focus on the great potentials. Approach your strategies objectively.

You may have realized you have plenty to learn when it comes to improving your communication and persuasion skills. Improvement is an ongoing process. You have to constantly and continuously work hard for it. More importantly, you have to be committed and dedicated.

Finally, you must always show respect. Keep in mind that you can only receive respect when you show respect. Always use a positive tone. Be tactful. Never use a condescending tone. Treat the other person as an equal. Be direct and show sincerity.

www.ingramcontent.com/pod-product-compliance
Lightning Source LLC
Chambersburg PA
CBHW070416190526
45169CB00003B/1283